Safe Kids
Fire Safety

Dana Meachen Rau

Marshall Cavendish Benchmark
New York

Never play with matches.

One small match can start
a big fire.

Do not get too close to fire.

Even candles can burn you.

Watch out for flames on the stove.

Your clothes can catch on fire.

Do not sit too close to
a *fireplace*.

Sparks can come out and
burn you.

Your house needs to have *smoke alarms*.

Beep! Beep! They warn you of a fire.

If you hear them beep,
leave the house.

A fire truck will hurry to
help you.

Practice a fire plan with your family.

You need two safe ways to get out.

Do not hide.

Firefighters need to find you.

Never open a hot door.

Feel your door first to see
if it is hot.

Smoke may fill the room.

Crawl out on the floor below the smoke.

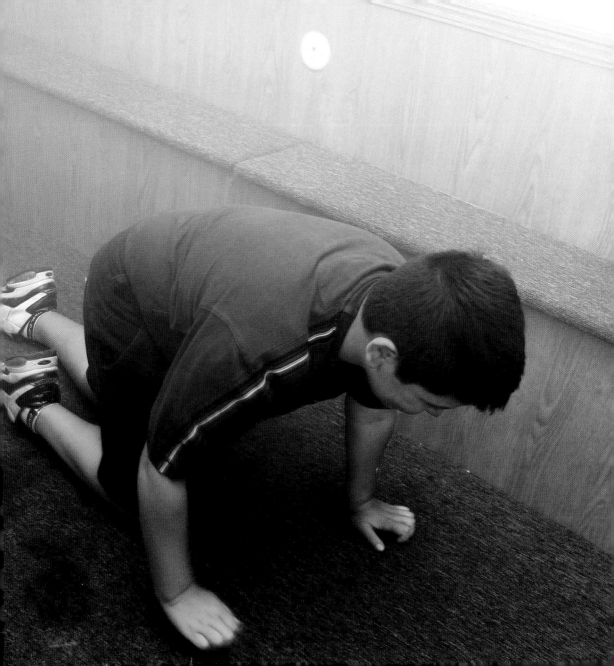

Your clothes could catch fire.

Stop, drop, and roll to put it out.

Have a safe place to meet your family outside.

Never go back into a fire.

Be a safe kid with fire.

Be Safe

candle

fire truck

fireplace

match

smoke

smoke alarm

stop, drop, and roll   **stove**

Challenge Words

fireplace A safe place to hold a fire that is built in a wall at the base of a chimney.

smoke alarm A machine that beeps loudly to show there is smoke from a fire.

Index

Page numbers in **boldface** are illustrations.

About the Author

Dana Meachen Rau is the author of many other titles in the Bookworms series, as well as other nonfiction and early reader books. She lives in Burlington, Connecticut, with her husband and two children.

With thanks to the Reading Consultants:

Nanci Vargus, Ed.D., is an Assistant Professor of Elementary Education at the University of Indianapolis.

Beth Walker Gambro is an Adjunct Professor at the University of Saint Francis in Joliet, Illinois.

31

Marshall Cavendish Benchmark
99 White Plains Road
Tarrytown, New York 10591-9001
www.marshallcavendish.us

Text copyright © 2010 by Marshall Cavendish Corporation

Library of Congress Cataloging-in-Publication Data

Rau, Dana Meachen, 1971-
Fire safety / by Dana Meachen Rau.
p. cm. — (Bookworms : Safe kids)
Includes index.
Summary: "Identifies common fire hazards and advises how to deal with them"
—Provided by publisher.
ISBN 978-0-7614-4091-8
1. Fire prevention—Juvenile literature. 2. Fires—Safety measures—Juvenile literature. I. Title.
TH9148.R44 2009
628.9'2—dc22
2008044931

Editor: Christina Gardeski
Publisher: Michelle Bisson
Designer: Virginia Pope
Art Director: Anahid Hamparian

Photo Research by Anne Burns Images

Cover Photo by *Photo Edit*/Myrleen Pearson

The photographs in this book are used with permission and through the courtesy of:
Getty Images: pp. 1, 11, 28BR Stephen Marks; p. 27 China Tourism Press.
Corbis: pp. 3, 28BL Chris Collins; pp. 9, 28TR Benelux/zefa; p. 25 James Leynse.
SuperStock: pp. 5, 28TL Photononstop; pp. 7, 29R Prisma; pp. 13, 19, 28TC age fotostock;
p. 17 SuperStock. *Photo Edit*: p. 15 Michael Newman; pp. 21, 28 Kayte Deioma;
pp. 23, 29L Richard Hutchings.

Printed in Malaysia (T)
3 5 6 4 2